The Sun and the Clouds

Bible Tales and Legends

The Sun and the Clouds

Bible Tales and Legends

by MENAHEM STERN

illustrations by

Ezekiel Schloss

KTAV PUBLISHING HOUSE INC.

SBN 87068-389-6

TABLE OF CONTENTS

To my son Arnold—with love.
The Author

Adam and the Animals

As the Lord was about to create the First Man, the birds and beasts were stirred by curiosity. They regarded each other with a puzzled look and asked: "Whom will the First Man resemble? To what extent will he be like us? And what good will he be to our community of birds and animals?"

The most curious and adventurous among them, the Eagle, Lion, Hyena, Fox and Dog, came to the site where the newly formed First Man lay, still without living breath in him. The first to have a good look at Man was the Eagle. He circled over the strange featherless body and, with his keen eyes he studied

the hands and feet, and expressed disappointment: "Of what use will Man be in my kingdom if he doesn't have any wings or feathers? Will he be able to escape an enemy in time, or migrate from one place to another in search of food and sunshine? Needless to say he will never know the pleasure of flying high over land and sea, of gliding effortlessly on soft blue winds. No! Such a helpless creature is surely not going to be one of my subjects and I haven't the slightest interest in him." Shrieking in mockery and anger, the Eagle disappeared into the far away. The Lion proudly stalked around the lifeless Man and muttered: "A poor defenseless creature. At night the cold will trouble him, and during the day the heat of the sun will scorch him. Any small animal will be able to destroy him. What an unworthy creature is coming into the world!" Then the Hyena thought the Man looked very funny and he burst into derisive laughter. But the clever Fox thought differently. With his shrewd eyes he studied Adam's clear forehead closely, the delicate pale cheeks and well-formed lips. He reflected sadly that Man looked superior to the animals and birds, and remarked: "I have been known as a wise creature. Big and small animals seek me out for advice. However, I can sense that when Man comes to life he will top everyone in wisdom and shrewdness." Humbly, with head bent downward, the Fox quickly left for the nearest thicket where the Lion and the Hyena had previously disappeared.

The only curious visitor who felt happy was the Dog, as he was lonely in the kingdom of animals. He sensed that nearby lay a devoted friend on whom one could depend for food, attention, and shelter. After the other animals had departed, the Dog sprang out from a surrounding clump of shrubs and, trembling with joy, leaped toward the still lifeless First Man. He sniffed, wagged his tail and cheerfully yelped as if trying to say something very important to Man who could not yet hear him.

At this very moment the sun came out from behind a cloud and poured down its most brilliant rays upon the earth. Not since the day of its creation had the sun shone so brightly. Its gleaming rays warmed the Man and caressed him, and he lay wrapped in light, for the Lord's countenance shone upon him. Thus life came into Adam and he breathed the pure invigorating air encompassing our earth.

And when Adam rose to his feet and for the first time looked at the beautiful world surrounding him, he was not lonely. Nearby stood the Dog, gazing upon his Master with boundless love and devotion.

Adam, Eve, and the Snake

When Adam and Eve were driven out of the Garden of Eden they found life very hard. They had to uproot trees in dense forests in order to farm the land or to graze their sheep and cattle on it. But above all they had to defend themselves against wild beasts which roamed the forests. No wonder that Adam and Eve were unhappy and restless and found it difficult to stay in one place for a long time.

They wandered constanly, dreaming that they would find a place where life would be as pleasant and easy as in the Garden of Eden.

One day they came to a river abundant with fish

and with many fruit trees growing on its shores. As if to please their sense of beauty, majestic mountains rose on the river's opposite bank.

For once Adam and Eve were favorably impressed by the pleasant countryside and by the abundance of food.

Still, they reminded themselves of the wonders of the Garden of Eden which they had so foolishly lost. When this happened, they felt a sadness oppressing them, but on second thought, they decided to settle in this lovely place and thus put an end to their wandering.

Meanwhile the snake, which had once slyly gotten Eve to eat the forbidden fruit, was lonely and glum in the Garden of Eden. One morning, as it stretched lazily in the sunlight, the snake was filled with self-pity.

"Because I am so clever," it thought, "I have nothing in common with any of the animals which live in the Garden of Eden. The only creatures whose company I found interesting were the two human beings who used to live here."

The snake felt a sudden stab of guilt.

"I feel sorry for Adam and Eve for leaving the pleasant life they enjoyed here. On the other hand—they must have gained from the hard life outside the Garden, for hardships sharpen the senses and the mind. In fact, they should be thankful to me. . . . But let me see for myself how the two humans are doing in the big world surrounding-our-island of easy, pleasant life—the Garden of Eden." And the snake grinned-in-self-satisfaction as it slithered into the-outside.

When one rainy afternoon the snake, after a long journey, came to the foot of a hill atop which stood the house of Adam and Eve, it blinked in bewilderment.

"What is this?" it gasped. For it had never before

seen a **house.** Then the idea that life within this building must be pleasant because it was sheltered from cold and rain flashed through the mind of the reptile, and deep envy of Adam and Eve surged through the snake.

"I started off as the most clever creature in the Garden. But now the humans are far ahead of me," angrily thought the snake. At once all its friendly feelings towards Adam and Eve were forgotten. Jealousy quickly grew into savage hatred and the snake started crawling up the hill with murder in its heart.

At this moment a huge dog, barking furiously, dashed out of the house.

The snake was ready to sink its poison into the dog when Adam rushed to the rescue. The man looked big and strong and the long heavy stick in his hand filled the snake with fear. After the snake had retreated from the hill it realized what a difference there was between man and itself. And it remembered the Lord's saying: "Human beings shall bruise your head any you shall bruise their heel."

And the snake slithered sadly away.

Cain

After Cain was cursed by the Lord for the murder of his brother Abel, he quickly picked up a few of his belongings and wandered away into the unknown. He walked a whole day without taking a rest, drinking, or eating. He was so busy walking that he hardly looked at the landscape. In the evening he felt very tired and his feet were sore from stepping on prickly plants. He plucked some grass and leaves and put them under his head, and he lay down to sleep at the foot of the nearest mountain. He tried in vain to fall asleep. He turned nervously from side to side. Finally he gave up the idea of falling asleep and re-

mained lying on his back, facing the low, dark-blue sky that was staring at him with many shiny stars. Two of the stars, the biggest and reddest, which were set close to the moon, resembled the eyes of his brother Abel and they seemed to ask: "Why did you kill me brother Cain? Didn't I help you to harvest your fields when you were ill? And, if you wished to have a lamb out of my flock for an offering of a sacrifice to God, wouldn't I let you have it? Were not my barn and stable always open to you? How could you commit such a terrible crime?"

Cain closed his eyes, but the stars seemed to shine through his eyelids and he could hear within him their silent yet powerful voices: "Why, brother Cain?" Suddenly, in the wind, he heard approaching steps. They had the same sound and rhythm as Abel's. . . . Fear gripped him. In his mind he saw the tall, mild-mannered Abel falling under the blow of the sharp-edged rock which he aimed at him with all his might. . . . And he thought regretfully, that the whole life of a human could depend on a single passion, on a quick moment. "Yesterday," he meditated, "my conscience was clear and I slept in a bed that was made up by the tender hands of mother Eve. Now I am a killer, a fugitive from my home and from my fertile land, with a mark on my forehead which reveals my terrible crime, and that I should be spared by an act of the Lord's mercy."

But he soon shook off the guilty thoughts and became again the hard, cruel Cain. "If not for that terrible thing—the sharp-edged stone that lay near me, Abel would still be alive . . . the feud would have ended in name-calling, abuses, as it always did . . . It is the devilish stone that prompted me to kill . . . The main guilt lies, therefore, with the stone and not with me . . ." he thought.

The stones and rocks on the mountain at whose foot Cain rested understood his thoughts and they became angry. "He blames the stone for the heinous murder instead of himself," exclaimed a stone bitterly. "A cowardly murderer! He refuses to face the truth which is the first step to repentance," said another stone. "Only for a short while was he soul-searching in honesty. Now he is again the same inhuman killer—Cain," came a third voice. The big rock that lay on the top of the mountain became agitated and shouted: "Cain is an abominable killer and as such he deserves to be destroyed. I will slide down from the top of the mountain and roll over him and kill him like a tiny fly."

"Hush! You can't kill Cain!" said the mountain, "for it is the will of God that the killer of his brother should remain alive! And you are not ordinary stones, for I am Mt. Sinai. One day Moses and the Hebrews whom he will liberate from Egyptian bondage will camp on the nearest plain. At the Lord's command Moses will go up to my top and, on a stone, he will engrave the Ten Commandments of which one will be: 'Do not kill!' "

The stones and rocks listened attentively to their Mountain, and didn't even stir.

The Nightingale and the Eagle

On that ominous morning crashing thunder wakened Noah from his sleep. He rushed to the window and watched the grim, ash-grey clouds moving over the sky. They seemed to have long, angry faces and deep cruel eyes. . . . In a short while the whole sky was one thick layer of clouds. "The flood is coming as the Lord said it would," thought Noah, and he carefully checked whether all creatures, male and female, were aboard the ark.

When he came to the bird section he saw the chirping sparrow, the plain wren, the proud peacock, the homely crow, and the fiery flamingo. Somehow, he felt that someone was missing

Ah, he thought, the lady nightingale is not here. I do not hear her lovely voice. Then he beheld the male nightingale and he knew that something was very much the matter. For the male nightingale was lonely and worried. He kept turning his restless, handsome head toward the entrance of the Ark.

Noah felt sorry and sent the male nightingale out to find his mate and hurry back to the Ark.

At this very moment Noah heard the beautiful sounds of a bird's song from a nearby orchard. He hastened to see who it was. On an old, blooming apple tree the female nightingale was singing a moving song of farewell to her lifelong friends, the tree and the orchard.

"Ho, there, my love!" the male nightingale was saying. "Please stop singing and get aboard the Ark. The flood is coming!"

But the lady nightingale paid no attention and went on singing.

Nervously, her mate pleaded with her: "You don't realize how serious the situation is, my dear! When the flood starts Noah will close the door of the Ark and . . . !" He wanted to tell his wife of the terrible fate that awaited all those who remained outside the Ark but the words stuck in his beak. His mate simply refused to listen and he flew back into the Ark in a state of despair.

Noah cast a worried glance at the clouds billowing in the sky. He had an idea. The bluejay is a noisy bird, he thought. No one can stand its loud screeching voice. A few good shrieks would make the nightingale realize that she'd better come into the Ark, at once.

So Noah sent out the bluejay. In a flash the clever bluejay was in the orchard. Settling himself on the old apple tree he broke into the nightingale's song with his harsh and shrieking voice. But the beautiful songstress was so busy performing that she paid no attention at all to the jay or his message.

When the bluejay returned alone, Noah was desperate: "A fine bird may be lost to the world and all

because it is so conceited," he mused.

Then his eyes lit up with a hopeful gleam as he spotted the eagle. "This is my last chance," said Noah as he sent the eagle on its important mission. When the nightingale saw the eagle with its powerful bill and sharp talons circling over the apple tree and shrieking out his message, she became panicky.

At the same time, however, she felt pleased, for she proudly thought: "Now I see what a good singer I am, for even the eagle has come to listen to my singing. Alas, he is too late; my song of farewell is at an end." And the songstress quickly flew into the Ark and joined her worried husband.

At this very moment the first giant drops of rain began to fall. Noah sighed. He was happy, but he was sad too. The eagle had done its task well, and yet a world was about to be lost. Regretfully, Noah stepped into the Ark and locked its doors.

Fish and Rainbow

When the waters of the flood covered every bit of earth, sand, and rock, turning our globe into one endless ocean, the world looked very sad.

Only the fish in the waters were happy. They stuck their heads out of the water, looked merrily around, and said to each other:

"Now our deadly enemies—the human beings—have all perished in the flood. From now on no one will ever spread nets for us, or catch us on sharp, iron hooks."

One day the fish saw a big wooden stucture floating on the water. It was Noah's Ark.

"What is this?" asked the smaller fish. The big, experienced fish stared with suspicion at the big Ark. They didn't know what to answer. They ordered a flying fish to circle over the Ark.

"People! People!" exclaimed the flying fish in despair when he returned from his flight. "With my own eyes did I see them!"

"I will bite through the bottom of this ugly vessel so that the water will pour in and drown these humans who have survived," said the mighty shark angrily.

He flung himself at the Ark and tried to sink his teeth in the wood. But in vain! The Ark was stronger than the shark's teeth.

"Nothing is as powerful and sharp as my sword!" triumphantly called out the swordfish, and he speedily rushed against the Ark.

Crash! The swordfish's sword hit against the hard wood of the Ark and broke in two!

The enormous whale murmured darkly: "As long as these few people remain alive there is no safety for us." With his body he tried to overturn the Ark. But even the whale was unsuccessful because the big and heavily-laden Ark was too strong for him.

The wise octopus, who was leading all the fish following the Ark, calmed down his brothers, speaking thus:

"Don't worry. Sooner or later the wood will rot in the water and the vessel will fall apart. There will be only water and sky!"

The octopus' words raised the spirits of the fish and they again rejoiced and frolicked as before.

One day the waters began to go down, and soon mountain peaks appeared.

On one peak Noah's Ark came to a halt. High above the mountain peak and the Ark, a beautiful, multicol-

ored rainbow appeared for the first time in the blue sky....

The fish became panicky: "Have the people in the Ark saved themselves? And what is this multicolored semicircle in the sky?"

In the depth of the seas lived the Leviathan, the wisest and oldest fish in the world. So all the fish swam down into the depths to find an answer.

The Leviathan looked at his fellow-fish with his big, sad eyes and in a soft voice he said:

"It is the will of God. Man remains the ruler of the rivers, lakes and seas, as well as of the dry land, and we fish must accept his rule. And the multicolored rainbow in the sky is a sign that there will never again be a flood on earth."

Since then, it is said that whenever fish see a rainbow in the sky they become sad and gloomy.

However, people—grown-ups and children alike—are happy, for they think about the Lord's promise to Noah.

The Sun and the Clouds

Shortly after God had created the world, the clouds saw that the sun was more appreciated and loved on earth than they were. That made them jealous and they said, "Of what use is the sun? How does it serve the earth and its inhabitants? Can it fill rivers, lakes, and ponds? Can the sun water the mountains and valleys, forests, gardens and fields as we, the clouds, do?"

Rumbling and grumbling, the clouds continued: "And see how proudly the sun rises in the sky! Such vanity! The only value the sun has is a rare beauty at dawn and at dusk which, we admit, can inspire the

poets on earth to write poems and the artists to paint pictures."

When the sun heard the insults of the clouds, it laughed a big round laugh and said, "Those gray, foolish clouds are so narrow-minded that they can't even understand that I, the sun, am the source of beauty and life on earth. If not for me, darkness and death would rule the world."

When the Great Flood came, the clouds cheered and their roaring laughter thundered in space. With wild glee they looked down upon the poor earth and joyfully watched how the waters, quickly rising, awesomely surging, swallowed houses, villages, and towns.

Loudly they proclaimed: "From now on we, the clouds, are more important than the sun. From now on, sunbeams will be useless, for the whole earth will turn into one sea."

The sun, its face hidden, felt very sad. It wandered from cloud to cloud, pleading, "For many days and nights you have kept the rain falling. By now the waters have covered all the earth and have probably destroyed all life. Please, clouds, forget your envy and hatred. Move aside so that my rays and warmth may reach the earth and dry it. Perhaps I will be able to save the few humans and other creatures who might still be alive."

But the clouds were so busy pouring water that they paid no attention. The pale sun thought glumly, "I have plenty of warmth and light for all of earth's creatures, for men, birds, beasts, and plants, but what can I do if the clouds block my way? And if no one will survive on earth what good am I? Who will need me and my golden rays?"

Just then the sun saw a huge multi-colored half-circle pierce the gray mass of clouds. The sun stared wonderingly at the beautiful arc. It was more colorful than blooming fields and meadows in springtime and more thrilling than the rushing waters of brooks and rivers flowing toward the sea on a bright summer evening.

The sun mustered its most friendly smile and asked uncertainly, "Would you please tell me who you are?"

"I am the rainbow, the sign of an agreement between God and man that no flood will ever destroy the earth," said the beautiful semicircle to the sun. "God has given His promise. As long as the earth lasts, every time the clouds gather for rain He will plant me, the rainbow, in the east for all to see and to remember the terrible flood."

"Does it really mean that all mankind has not been destroyed by the flood?" cried the sun. "How wonderful!"

At that moment a powerful wind started blowing. It scattered the clouds, and allowed the sun's golden rays to dry the soaking earth. And the Ark's passengers came out and stretched their weary limbs, and trees and flowers and food-bearing plants began to grow.

Since then the clouds have often felt ashamed of themselves. But the sun has forgiven them over and over again.

The Bottom of the Well

After journeying for three days, Abraham and his son Isaac came to the foot of a hill in the land of Moriah. Tired and sad, they sat down on a flat rock and were silent. Abraham thought how close he was to fulfillment of God's voice within him. After a short rest they would ascend the hill where he would sacrifice his beloved son. . . .

At this thought his right hand, which held a big, sharp knife, trembled violently and his heart sank.

"How horrible! How can I kill my own child?" he thought. Abraham saw himself as an evil man without human feelings, smitten by guilt, wandering like

Cain from place to place in shame and disgrace to avoid familiar faces of beloved relatives, friends, and acquaintances. Then he thought of his kind wife Sarah: Through all the days of talk and preparation before the journey she had innocently believed that a lamb would be sacrified. She was never aware that her beloved son was destined to be a burnt-offering. But when they were ready to go, her face had saddened with pain and pity and tears had poured down her cheeks.... How shocked she would be to hear the sad news! Would she ever forgive this cruel and shameful deed? Then like a flame in dry brush the idea came to him that all he was doing was because of God's will and, if God wanted Isaac to be sacrificed, he must obey. Abraham's thoughts continued with warmth and zeal: "Did I refuse to obey the Lord's voice when He spoke to me in the idol-worshipping land of my birth and commanded me to leave the comfort of my home and settle in the unknown land of Canaan? Is not the will of the Lord more important even than my own child's life?"

These thoughts gave him vigor and courage and Abraham regained his calm and his conscience stopped gnawing at him when he thought of the horror which awaited his beloved son.

Now, near his father sat the boy Isaac, and he seemed so small as he looked with sad, bewildered eyes at the hill rising in front of him. Isaac beheld the landscape covered with short prickly bushes; he squinted at the grass and yellow stones parched by the scorching sun and at the cloudless sky crowning the hilltop. He said to himself, "The blue sky and the hill look so peaceful but I am very sad, for my father doesn't pay any attention to me. He was always kind and warm-hearted but now he behaves like a stranger. I asked my father about a lamb for a sacrifice,

and he answered that the Lord would provide. Now we are already at the foot of the hill, yet there is no trace of a lamb. What can it all mean?"

The lad cast a fearful glance at the large, sharp knife in Abraham's hand and at the flaming torch leaning against a nearby rock. A wild thought entered his mind: "What if I ran away and hid in the fields and forests surrounding the hill? If my life is in danger, a few quick steps into the thick brush and I'd be safe!"

Isaac looked eagerly at the wide valley covered with tall grass, with colorful flowers, with bushes and trees. A great longing to live welled up in the lad. Then a new thought, more forceful than the other, came into his mind: "No! I will not run awav. The God of my father is also **my** God and if it is His will that I should die on the altar, I will not hesitate and I will die courageously."

"Father!" Isaac cried in a firm voice. Abraham, who by now was in a state of deep religious feeling, listened as if the voice came from afar: "The flowers in the valley are very beautiful. Allow me to pick some, and in case I don't return home you will give them to my beloved mother."

"Yes . . . yes . . . do so, my son," replied Abraham in a gruff voice not his own.

As the lad plucked the tender violets, daisies, and roses, he thought how his dear mother would love their smell and touch, for they would remind her of him, her beloved son, born to her when she was already old. He reminded himself of a story his mother had told him in happier days, a tale of three wanderers who, after being welcomed with food and drink, blessed his parents and said that they would have a son.

"I burst out laughing," his mother had told him,

"for I couldn't believe that at my age I would beget a child. Well, my dear, you are the son who was born to us a year later and because of my laughter we named you Yitzhak."

Now Isaac's courage and inner strength had drained away and tears streaked his soft cheeks and moistened the petals and stalks of the flowers in his hands. Then, behind a dense cluster of rosebushes, Isaac discovered a well; it was over-grown with tall grass and weeds, for it had been forgotten by nomads and shepherds. The lad bent over its moss-covered edge and stared into the deep well, and the water way down looked dark-green and scummy. Suddenly his mother's face appeared on the water's surface, the features distorted with pain and her eyes red from crying.

"Mother! Mother!" Isaac cried into the cool depths of the ancient well. He could not utter more than this single word, which was a call for help and protection in this bitter moment. Then, to his great surprise, the dark-green water was suddenly set a-sparkle by a sunray which shafted into the well, and Sarah's face lost its look of pain and was alight with a gay, kind smile. Then the lad heard his mother's soft, reassuring voice rising from the bottom of the well.

"I have prayed for you, my son. Have no fear, for the Lord will save and protect you."

"Thank you, Mother, thank you," whispered Isaac and strength surged through his whole being. From the foot of the hill came Abraham's faraway voice: "Soon the day will be gone; come, son, let us ascend the hill and fulfill the Lord's wish."

Abraham quickly built the altar, laid out the split pieces of kindling-wood, and tied his son and put him on the pyre. Isaac felt no pain as the thin rope cut into his flesh. Though he heard the angry hissing of the torch and saw the big knife lifted high in his father's hand, glinting in the setting sun, the iron blade ready to press its weight on his neck, he lay fearless and confident in his belief in the mercy of the Creator.

At this very instance Abraham put away the knife, as the Lord had commanded him to do. With quick, nervous gestures he took Isaac off the altar and freed his hands and feet. "The Lord is all-merciful. He does not want human sacrifices. He only tested my devotion to Him." murmured the father in a broken voice full of emotion, as he hugged and kissed his son.

"Yes, Father, the Lord **is** all-merciful," whispered Isaac as he looked up in gratitude. Once again tears flowed from his eyes, but this time they were tears of boundless joy.

Esau Prepares a Meal for His Father Isaac

Esau took his bow and arrows and hurried through the uneven paths of the little village, past large, breezy tents and gray shacks with windows as small as holes, from some of which came a blue smoke that filled the air with the flavor of baked and cooked food. Soon he came across calm, ploughed glens and sparse clusters of fig and olive trees. As the last trace of the village path disappeared in the midst of tall grass and stones and a colorful, untamed vista of forests, plains and rocks engulfed him, Esau grinned with satisfaction. Tall, robust, and hairy, he walked briskly through grass and bushes, at times kicking at a pebble and watching it bounce along. He reached for blades of grass, felt their soft freshness and vigor and contentedly thought: "This summer the grass is tall and full, as there was a lot of rain and the deer meat is surely juicy and tasty. Father Isaac will be pleased with the meal I'll have ready for him and he will bless me as his first-born son with his very best blessings." And he dreamed of how his father's blessings would give him inner strength and increase his prestige in the eyes of the inhabitants of the area; of how the blessings should help him realize his ambitions to become a powerful leader of a new nation. As his grandfather Abraham became the founder and chief of a great nation, abundant in wealth and brave in war, of which all other nations and tribes were afraid, so would he also triumph.

A short while later Esau came to the bank of a brook where he hid in a clump of bushes that blended with the surrounding branches and leaves. With his bow and arrows poised, he tensely waited for a fawn or a young deer to come to drink from the water of the brook. But despite a long, silent wait, none appeared. He began to panic, while this thought ran through his mind: "Suppose my old feeble father dies without blessing me—what then? Mother Rebecca never had a deep love for me, and she would even more openly favor her beloved Jacob, that placid, meditative stay-at-home who hangs onto her skirt. Sooner or later I would have to leave home!" At the thought of his brother Jacob he felt greatly irritated. In his mind he saw Jacob's sensitive face, keen, warm eyes, legs and arms that were quite strong, though neglected by living a domesticated, tamed life which he abhorred. "A vigorous man but what a waste!" And he thought how they quarreled and fought with each other and how once in the field, while no one was

around, he had suddenly grabbed Jacob and tried to push him down into a ravine————

Just then a bush to to his left shook, and two young deer crossed the path and silently scampered toward the brook to quench their thirst. However, Esau was so busy thinking and dreaming that he forgot the purpose of his coming there and didn't notice the animals.

"Of all my relatives I most admire grandfather Abraham for his outstanding courage and devotion to an ideal," he went on thinking. "He left his close kin and homeland and wandered to strange far-off regions. But he was no hunter, no man with a savage beat in his blood. Whenever he happened to take a walk in the field or forest, he did so not to satisfy his primitive instincts, not to unite with raw nature. Grandfather Abraham isolated himself from people to talk with God. . . . And there's another thing I don't like about him—his protectiveness of the weak and the doomed, which is not to my taste. I have learned that in the field and forest the strong attack and eat the weak and that is the way it always was in nature and always will be. But grandfather Abraham behaved contrary to nature's laws. He even debated with God trying to save the people of Sodom and Gomorrah from the fire of destruction. What an odd individual he was!"

Suddenly Esau was shocked by the sight of the sun which had passed the center of the sky in its path to the west. The bushes, stones, and earth showed a silvery tinge in the calm afternoon. "My old sick father is waiting for me and I, excellent hunter that I am, have been wasting my time dreaming," he feverishly thought.

Esau slipped out of the tangle of bushes and walked alongside the brook. From behind a rocky hillside a young deer darted toward a line of short, heavy-set thickets that hung around a glen, not far from Esau. The animal ran with lightning speed, its eyes glowing, phosphorescent with fear. Obviously it was separated from its mother in flight from a wild beast. Esau raised his bow and shot a deadly arrow into its hot, trembling body. Back home again, he set about preparing a tasty meal out of the deer's meat. But on entering his father's room he was met by the shocking news that Jacob his younger brother, had already been blessed. His rage was so great that he vowed to kill Jacob.

Joseph in the Dungeon

The jail cell into which the Egyptian guards had put Joseph on the false accusations of Potiphar's wife was small and dirty. Little light, still less sunshine, seeped in through the single small window covered with heavy iron bars. The pencil strokes of light fell upon the gray walls and the group of prisoners of whom Joseph was now one.

Distressed by injustices and a prisoner in a strange land, the handsome lad sat in a corner lonely and downcast and dreamed of his loving father and of the beautiful land of Canaan, its cool springs, singing rivers and brooks. He thought of the peaceful

valleys and hills where he used to graze his father's flocks of sheep.

Suddenly his daydream was broken by the hoarse voice of a fellow prisoner.

"Ho, there! What brought **you** in here?"

Joseph looked at the man who had asked the question. He had long, bony hands and a rough face from which stared two shrewd eyes. Most of the prisoners burst into laughter, for they expected to enjoy a quarrel between a hardened prisoner and the new arrival with the tender, innocent face. Joseph turned toward them and coolly looked at the odd-looking figure. "What a wretched, rough face," he thought.

"Are you a thief or a murderer?" the prisoner cried. He was playing to his audience now and they waited eagerly for a reply.

"Neither!" answered Joseph with dignity.

"An honest man wouldn't be here," shouted a prisoner with a black patch over his right eye.

"That's right!" chorused the others with bitter glee.

Two burly men who had been sitting near the window in serious discussion got up and came close to Joseph. A few days ago one had been the baker and the other the butler in Pharaoh's palace. Both had been jailed for offending the ruler. They felt that Joseph could not defend himself and angrily shouted, "Leave him in peace! Get away from him!" Outnumbered, the prisoner moved away from Joseph.

One day, when Joseph felt more disheartened than ever by the harsh jail life and by the intolerant behavior of some of the prisoners, he went over to the small window. His eyes caught sight of a swallow flying to and fro and yet never disappearing from his eye. The bird reminded him of freedom, of his kind father Jacob, and of Canaan's green pastures.

He wished that he had the freedom of the bird so that he might be able to fly from one country to another. How swiftly he would have flown to his beloved home!

And behold, at this very instant as if the swallow understood his thoughts, it flew toward the little window with the heavy bars against which Joseph's tired head rested. It fluttered upon the edge of the window sill and called out, "Tweet, tweet! I've just come from your beautiful homeland where I saw your father Jacob and your brothers. Your old father is in deep grief for he thinks that you are dead. Your brothers deeply regret the disgraceful deed they committed against you in a rash moment of envy."

Joseph broke into tears and cried out: "Swallow, dear swallow, fly to my beloved father and dear brothers and tell them that I am alive and that with all my heart and soul I yearn to be united with them." In a flash the swallow disappeared, flying northward over the sandy wasteland of the Sinai Peninsula toward Canaan's lovely hills and glens.

Then Joseph looked up. A stray sunbeam filtered into the cell and touched his face. Around him lay the ragged companions who shared his miserable fate. They slept heavily. At this moment a strange feeling of happiness came over him as he thought that some day he would be reunited with his family.

The River Nile and the Waters of the Sea

When the old, proud Mediterranean Sea discovered that new-born Hebrew boys were thrown into the River Nile it became very angry and exclaimed:

"Waters! Of all the rivers which flow into me the Nile brings shame and disgrace upon me. From now on I shall have nothing in common with Egypt's biggest river in whose waters Hebrew babies are drowned. I shall keep the Nile away and not mingle with its waters and waves.

"How horrible! How shocking! Away! Away!" shrieked the waters of the Mediterranean, swelling high and strong like a mighty wall and thus keeping

the Nile as close to the shore as possible.

The Nile waters felt deeply offended. They slowly flowed in silence and humiliation. After a while they spoke up in a low but clear voice:

"We bring happiness to Hebrew and Egyptian alike by watering the sun-scorched pastures and farmlands of Egypt. Is it fair to accuse us of such atrocious deeds? Is it our fault that Hebrew babies are carried off from their loving parents by the guards of the cruel Pharaoh and thrown into us? Do we have to pay for human cruelties?"

The Mediterranean Sea ordered its waters and waves to be calm for a moment. It meditated and said:

"Perhaps so. . . . The fact, nevertheless, remains that in your waters newborn babies lose their lives."

The Nile muttered and moaned in protest.

"Please do listen to reason," it said. But its pleading voice was lost in a storm of shrieks and shouts by the now aroused waves and waters of the Mediterranean Sea.

When the Lord saw how sad and dejected the waters of the Nile were, He felt pity for the river and spoke thus:

"The River Nile is surely right in saying that it doesn't have to pay for cruelties committed by human beings, for Pharaoh and his people are the perpetrators of evil and not the river. I shall therefore repay the Nile for the humiliation and disgrace thus endured and it will become the cradle of Jewish hopes and salvation. For a baby boy of the tribe of Levi will find safety on its waters and, one day, he will be chosen as My servant and the Liberator and Law Giver of the Hebrew people."

As the waters of the Mediterranean Sea listened to what the Lord had spoken they became calm and from then on they have gladly accepted the Nile River into their midst.

The Bush

In an oasis, amid tall and beautiful trees, grew a frail bush. The leaves on its thin branches were few and dry and its fruit was puny and stunted.

Wandering Bedouins who used to stop in the oasis plucked the fruit from the well-nourished trees, ate heartily, and rested in the cool shade of their fragrant boughs. But no one came to the small, frail bush. Yet the hot desert breezes did not pass it by. The cruel winds beat against the bush with all their might in an effort to uproot it.

The young tree, aware of its weakness and skimpy size, felt downhearted and asked:

"Why am I the frailest of all bushes and trees in the oasis? What have I done that my lot is so hard?"

"That's how things are in this world," harshly answered the big trees. And after their answer the bush felt even more melancholy than before.

One day a searing tongue of fire descended from the sky and enveloped the bush. The young bush was terrified. It rustled its branches and called out in despair:

"Now I am lost! Fire is more destructive than the desert wind, more painful than loneliness, more shameful than dry branches. The fire will put an end to me!"

Then the fire lit up with a brightness which was greater than the brightness of the sun. It spoke:

"Do not fear, bush, for I am not the fire which consumes. I am the fire of the eternal God, the God of love and mercy. And soon you will see and hear things which no tree on earth has ever seen or heard."

The young bush wanted to say something but it was unable to utter a word for it was filled with awe. It could only bow deeply, and brush the ground with low-hanging branches.

Then, through the thin veil of glowing flame, it looked about with curiosity.

At the foot of a hill a shepherd was grazing a flock of sheep. The bush saw the shepherd stare in surprise and in wonder, for the fire was burning ceaselessly, and yet the bush was not consumed.

The shepherd left his flock and came closer and the bush could see his keen-eyed, marvelling face, and his jaw hanging slack with amazement.

At this instant the voice of God spoke from the fire, saying:

"Moses! Moses! Take off your shoes for the ground

on which you stand is holy."

"How miraculous!" whispered the bush. "Not once in all my life have I experienced an event like this. And who could have known that the soil on which I grow is holy ground!" And again the bush bowed low.

The bush grew quickly silent as the Lord's voice again spoke to the shepherd, telling him to go to Pharaoh, the ruler of Egypt, and order him to let the Children of Israel free.

When Moses had left, the Lord spoke again from the crackling fire. This time He spoke to the bush:

"You have found grace in My eyes and therefore have you seen and heard Me as I spoke to My faithful servant Moses. Rejoice in your lot, bush, and let no blazing desert sun, sweeping sandstorm nor weakness of branches trouble you."

And as the Lord finished speaking the great flame disappeared.

From that day on the bush was content with its lot, for it knew that it had fulfilled a great mission in the history of the world.

The Date Tree

On the shore of the River Nile grew a tall, beautiful date tree. The tree grew happily for it had water in abundance and the cool breezes blowing from the river refreshed its deep-green leaves on hot summer days. Perhaps because of its happiness it greeted every wanderer who happened to come under its pleasant shade with a cheerful rustle of its branches, whispering: "Welcome, welcome."

One day came Pharaoh's order to throw Jewish new-born boys into the Nile. Brutal Egyptians ran into Jewish homes, snatched the male babies from their mothers' breasts and threw them into the river.

The path along which the guards strode with the snatched babies to the river led through the place where the date tree stood.

Each time the tree saw a Hebrew child being carried off by an Egyptian guard to the Nile it sadly shook its branches in protest:

"Woe that I have to see such cruelties! Pharaoh's guards, how low you have fallen!"

Yet despite its sadness and grief the date tree grew even taller and lovelier than before and its fruits grew juicier and bigger.

One day as Pharaoh took a walk along the Nile's shore he saw the beautiful date tree. Being a lover of trees and plants he ordered the date tree transplanted into his own garden. This his servants quickly did. From then on the date tree stood in a beautiful spot in the garden of Egypt's ruler; yet it continued to be as unhappy as before.

"How can I enjoy living in Pharaoh's garden when Hebrew babies are drowned in the River Nile?" it thought.

One day heavy clouds covered Egypt's skies and big hailstones fell upon city and village, hill and valley, garden and field, as a punishment for the enslavement of the Hebrews. When the Egyptians looked out of their homes they saw a horrible sight as all the fields, vineyards, and gardens were destroyed. The same devastation had taken place in Pharaoh's garden.

As Egypt's mighty ruler peered out through a palace window he saw that the trees and bushes were leafless and all the beautiful flowers lay on the ground as if a giant had walked over them. Only one tree stood green and fresh as before and that was the date tree which his servants had recently transplanted.

For a while Pharaoh was glad.

"The God of Moses and Aaron isn't as powerful as they claim Him to be. One of my trees is mightier than the plague," he thought. But then a feeling of fear overwhelmed him and a new idea came to him.

"The date tree is unlike all other trees, so the heavy hailstones could not destroy its fruit and leaves. The thing is not so simple and there is surely more meaning to it than appears on the surface." And he ordered his wise men to look into this matter.

The wise men thought and then said: "Your Majesty the King! The date tree symbolizes the Hebrews, for as the hail could not destroy its leaves and fruits, so can we not destroy the Hebrew people, nor their spirit, nor their love for freedom. In vain are the cruelties and oppression we inflict upon them. Let the King therefore restore their freedom and forbid cruel acts against them."

Pharaoh was impressed by the wisdom of the wise men and he sent for Moses and Aaron and asked them to pray to God to stop the hailstones, for he was ready to set the Hebrews free.

However, when Moses and Aaron had prayed to God and the hailstorm ceased, Pharaoh changed his mind and again decided not to let the Hebrews free.

The Falling Pyramid

Pharaoh, the King of Egypt, wanted to impress his own high officials, as well as those of neighboring lands, with his country's tallest pyramid. Therefore, he ordered the Hebrew slaves to build a pyramid as high as possible so that no other pyramid or building in Egypt and abroad would be able to match it. The Hebrew stone-cutters and builders worked day and night, as they were ordered to build it at great speed.

During the day they worked under the scorching Egyptian sun and through the nights they toiled by torchlight. More than one Hebrew was crushed by a heavy rock while building under the sharp eyes of the severe taskmasters who demanded more and more work. When the pyramid was finished Pharaoh gave a big feast, to which he invited his distinguished guests. At the base of the pyramid, at tables covered with exquisite drinks and tasty dishes, sat the important guests, while musicians played cheerful tunes to stimulate their appetite for eating and drinking.

Between the courses smooth, well-trained toastmasters raised their cups of drink in honor of Egypt's king and in honor of the tallest pyramid on earth. They praised Pharaoh's great skill in building and his talent in administration. Pharaoh felt very proud.

While the Egyptian king and his guests were at the peak of their merrymaking, a Hebrew man struggled desperately inside the pyramid to break out. During the speedy working hours of the previous night in the faint glow of torchlight,he was busy cementing the inside of the stony colossus. Because of poor food and hard work the man became very tired and fell asleep. This was a very bad time to choose for sleeping, for the last stone bricks were being filled into the wall and the sleeping man remained a hopeless prisoner engulfed by dark, heavy walls of stone. When the Hebrew slaves realized that Hanoch (for that was his name) was missing, thev demanded that a stone brick be taken out of the wall of the pyramid, and that someone should go in to look for their friend. But the cruel taskmaster refused and the Hebrews, under the terror of whips, stricken by grief and pain, had to leave tearfully for their homes.

Hanoch slept for many hours, until the cheerful music, laughter, and noise of the drunken guests praising Pharaoh for building this gigantic piece of architecture—the tallest pyramid—woke him from his sleep. He slowly realized what had happened and the danger he was in. At first he felt desperate and saw himself dying a slow death within the walls of the pyramid—the very pyramid the officials and dignitaries were praising so loudly. But Hanoch, though weakened through lack of food and fresh air, was not the kind of man to give up without a struggle.

In the darkness he felt for his tools and started to

scrub off the cement joining the stone bricks, the cement he had used the previous night and which now cut him off from light, from his family and people. Only on the surface was it dry, stone dry, but deep inside the cement was still freshly wet. Hanoch worked with all the determination and strength he had left.

Suddenly there was a rumble as if stone to stone spoke in their language; the wall collapsed and an ear-splitting noise was heard. Then the other walls, lacking support, crumbled and fell with a thunderous crash. The whole mighty pyramid lay in one huge pile of stone, rubble and dust under which lay the Hebrew slave, Hanoch, and most of Pharaoh's guests.

Egypt's king was alive and unhurt. For a while he was paralyzed with fear. Then, gloomy and soiled, his knees shaking, he stepped into his chariot and left for the palace. In shame and anger he thought: "What will the kings and rulers say of me? Pharaoh is a show-off, a buffoon not a king. He invites our ministers and dignitaries to be buried under his falling pyramids!"

Walking nervously back and forth in the palace, Pharaoh thought with bitter hatred of Moses and Aaron, who endlessly vexed him with their demands for freedom of the Jewish people.

"It is certainly a Hebrew plot!" he exclaimed to his wise men who stood in a corner of the room and fearfully eyed the king. One of them, however, the bravest and the oldest, who knew the truth and had courage, said: "Your honor! Let the Hebrews free! For what happened to the pyramid might some day happen to our country."

But Pharaoh, who was known for his stubbornness, would not listen to his advice and went on ill-treating the oppressed Hebrews.

Pharaoh Was Afraid of the Dark

The plague of darkness that hit Egypt put a deep fear into the hearts of the Egyptians.

Most frightened of all was Pharaoh. Shifting nervously on his throne, he thought: "With the exception of the frogs, which were more of a nuisance than a disaster, the plagues have done a lot of harm to my country. But—darkness! This calamity will undermine the devotion of my people. My spies tell me of wide discontent—yet I can't give in to Moses and Aaron who speak in the name of an invisible God. Besides, the mighty priests of Apis will say that Pharaoh, the son of heaven, is a weakling and cow-

ard! No! I **must** keep the Hebrews in slavery!"

At this very moment, the noise of breaking glass shattered the silence. A servant, feeling his way toward the King with refreshments, had slipped and the glass had fallen out of his hand.

"Horrible darkness!" muttered Pharaoh.

Then he slowly stepped down from the throne and, without anyone's assistance, felt his way out from the palace. Poking ahead with his staff and taking small, careful steps, Pharaoh moved through the silent, deserted streets. But when he had calmed down and wished to return, he couldn't find his way back and wandered still farther from the palace.

As he walked on, confused and forlorn, he found himself in front of a house. The door opened and a man took Pharaoh by the hand and led him into the house. The King felt as if the house were filled with the brightness of a summer's day flowing in through the window like a silver stream of water. A Jewish home, he thought, for the Jews were not affected by the plague.

"You have obviously lost your way, O King. Be seated and rest," said the man who had led him in, in a polite voice.

At the other end of the room, a young woman sat on a low chair. Her face was pale, her eyes were red and wet with tears, and her uncombed hair lay loosely upon her shoulders.

Pharaoh gaped at the young woman who sat motionless and heedless of his presence.

"We lost our only son a few nights ago," said the man. "Your soldiers came and carried off our child and threw him into the Nile."

"How dreadful! How shocking!" cried Pharaoh. "I will stop this barbaric practice immediately and I will punish those who drowned your son."

As the King, with the help of his Jewish guide, went back to the palace, he thought of how good his father had been to the Hebrews and how wicked he had been to them since he became King.

"As soon as Moses and Aaron will remove the darkness I will let the Jews free," he said to himself. But when Moses and Aaron took away the darkness, Pharaoh did not free the Jews, nor did he stop throwing new-born boys into the Nile.

Then a more severe plague came—the one that killed the first-born boys in all Egyptian families. Then, only then, did Pharoah free the Jews.

A Legend of the Red Sea

When the news reached the King of the Red Sea that the Egyptians were pursuing the Israelites, he rose from his coral throne and said to the waters:

"Moses has freed the children of Israel. But Pharaoh hopes to drive the Israelites into the sea. To save themselves, the Israelites must cross our waters.

"Now hear my instructions, waters! Make a path, so that Moses and his people will be able to reach the shore safely."

Most of the waters were in favor of helping the Children of Israel. They bubbled happily and cried in excitement:

"We waters love freedom and endless space, so we know what freedom means to the Hebrews. We will gladly fulfill your wish, O King."

But some of the waters opposed the King's orders. They foamed angrily and roared:

"Why should we be good to human beings? They don't care about us! Let them build boats and sail to safety in **them** if they can!"

The obedient, helpful waters spoke patiently and wisely:

"Don't you know what happened in Egypt? Because Pharaoh was so stubborn and wicked, God turned all the waters in Egypt to blood. Would you want the same fate to happen to us?"

The uncooperative waters grew even angrier at this. "The sea is for fishes and pearls and not for human beings. We shall never allow ourselves to be parted just so that people may walk through us!"

But the good waters refused to give up. Their waves lapped quietly as they used every means of persuasion. They said:

"Our distant relative, the river Nile, once carried a basket in which lay the baby Moses. Now Moses, the Liberator, and his people have come to our shore. Will we suddenly become merciless? Shall we not divide and make a way until all the men, women, and children have reached safety?"

The bad waters did not know how to answer, so they contented themselves by swelling up, roaring fiercely, and slapping their wild waves against the peace-loving waters.

The Red Sea became very stormy. The old King of the Red Sea rushed to the surface. With watery eyes he wept as he saw multitudes of fearful, desperate Hebrews and, far behind them, in a cloud of dust,

Pharaoh's war chariots, rushing madly towards their prey.

At this moment, Moses, leader of his people, stepped out from among the great throng of Israelites and lifted his staff. A historic event was to take place.

"Some of my waters are merciless and disobedient. I must help the Children of Israel or they will perish!" thought the old King of the Red Sea. And he called for the mightiest winds to help him divide the sea.

The winds swooped down upon the waters.

"I brought the locusts upon the Egyptian fields and gardens and I am now ready to help the Israelites against their enemies!" screamed one wind.

"And I"—roared another wind—"I drove the hail-clouds over the towns and villages of Egypt."

Now both winds lashed the bad waters with all their fury. And lo, the wicked waters were parted from the good waters so that the Red Sea split widely, and a path was opened in the heart of the sea.

And as Moses and the Children of Israel trod the dry path that led them to safety, the old King of the Red Sea sat on his coral throne and a smile of satisfaction played upon his face.

The Sand and the Rocks

Soon after God created the world a terrible windstorm arose and swept a great heap of sand into the air. Tiny specks of golden sand whirled through space. Soon they came to a river with a beautiful garden on its banks.

Said the specks of sand: "The river and trees are lovely indeed. But they cannot be compared with **us**. For is it not better to be able to hover in space and move when one wishes and see rivers, mountains, and gardens from a great height?"

When the garden and the river heard this they felt very offended.

"Those tiny specks of sand consider themselves superior to us!" said they. "Ha!" said an oak tree.

"What's more," complained a birch tree, "the golden rays of the sun can't even reach my branches and my leaves because of the dust cloud."

"Quite a nuisance," rustled some bushes.

Before long, all the trees, and even the lowly shrubbery in the garden, were protesting and complaining. They waved their twigs and branches furiously as if by doing so they could drive away their uninvited guest.

And what did the river do? When it saw how the wind was blowing and what the general feeling was, it grew restless and bulged with anger. Powerful, muttering waves dashed wrathfully against the river banks.

The specks of sand saw that they were not welcome so they shrugged and moved on. After wandering aimlessly for some time they came over a mountain. The mountain stood solemnly and full of majesty, raising its bulk against a hot desert plain and a clear blue sky.

Its slopes, dotted with scrubby bushes and grass, spread upward toward a barren flat top covered with huge rocks. The specks of sand peered closely at the rocks and said: "What huge rocks! What an odd beauty they have! Anyone who loves beautiful things ought to see them."

But after they had studied the rocks more carefully, the sandspecks murmured:

"Alas, there is not a single sign of life on them, and not a plant or herb sprouts from them. Neither rain, nor wind, nor sun, nor moon has the slightest effect on them. They endure a miserable existence. Ah, what a pity that the poor mountain must carry those rocks!"

When the rocks heard the remarks made by the cloud-of-sand, they sent up a chorus of complaint to God.

"Lord of the Universe," they said, "You have created us by Your will. Is it our fault no plant or herb can grow from us? These tiny specks of sand have come and brought us shame and embarrassment!"

Immediately the wind that bore aloft the specks of sand ceased to blow and every speck of sand dropped to the desert plain. Now it was eerily silent and not a thing moved.

Through the stillness came a great and booming sound, loud as a thousand thunderclaps and edged with the sharpness of lightning.

And God spoke: "Do not feel any shame, rocks! Rejoice, for your home is on the very top of Mount Sinai. Some day the Children of Israel will be set free from Egyptian slavery. They will set out for the Promised Land and in their wandering they will one day pitch their tents and camp at the foot of this mountain which is your dwelling-place.

"And My servant Moses will climb to the top of the mountain, which men will call Sinai, and stay there for forty days and forty nights. And on one of your rocks he will engrave My Ten Commandments!"

Thus the humble rocks learned that they had a great mission to fulfill on earth.

There was silence again, but now the rocks rejoiced and they glinted in the golden rays of the sun as they had never before.

Deborah and Her Acacia Tree

Among the Hebrew wanderers who had left Egypt and were on the way to the Promised Land was Dan, a man in the early thirties, tall and strongly built, and his daughter of eleven, Deborah.

Each time Dan looked at his daughter's pale, thin face and brown sunken eyes, telling of the many hardships met by the Hebrews in the desert he was reminded of his wife Melka, a smiling, good-natured woman who, at the start of the long journey, had been bitten by a poisonous snake and had died. Since then the father had loved his frail daughter with a double love and had protected her as much as ever he could from the angry elements of the wilderness.

One evening when the wanderers were resting after a hard day of walking in the scorching heat, Deborah was gazing with sad eyes at the flames rising from the pile of crackling branches and logs of wood in front of them and, not turning her face towards her father, she asked impatiently:

"Father, how long do we still have to wander through the desert? When shall we come into the Land of Canaan?"

Her father protectively patted Deborah's soft hair with his strong, hard hand and said:

"We still have a long way to go daughter, but with God's help we shall arrive there."

The girl sighed and her eyes were unhappy.

To their right people were talking loudly, arguing passionately; obviously the matter was of the utmost importance to them. To their left and in front, people munched on food or lay asleep in various positions, and in the rear they were screened by a group of rocks. From far away, past multitudes of shacks, human bodies, and fires came the sad howling of a jackal. It was soon drowned out by the rhythmic singing of vigorous, youthful voices:

Cool water in the well,
How precious you are
I cannot tell . . .

The frail, sensitive girl wasn't cheered by the vigorous, rhythmic voices. The enormous heat of the day and the melancholy of the desert evening lay heavy upon her. Her father took a handful of figs out of his bag and put them before his daughter.

"Eat Deborah, the figs are superb . . . they will give you strength and raise your spirits." Dan said softly

and pleadingly. But the girl moved them aside and said:

"Father, I am tired of endless wandering over stones and sand. I love grass, flowers, and trees and I like to live, not in a wind-torn hut but in a real house, with a solid roof, door, and windows, like the ones they have in Egypt . . ."

Dan threw a surprised glance at his daughter for he had never heard her speak like that. He was ready to reprimand her harshly but seeing her sickly, pale face his whole being was overcome by compassion and he spoke softly but with deep conviction.

"Better the sands and stones of the desert than the fertile pastures of Goshen, Deborah. Here we are a free people, with no Pharaoh and his pack of taskmasters over us. We are led by the great liberator and teacher Moses and, ahead of us, like a pillar of fire at night is the promise of a land of honey and milk."

Deborah watched her father's small eyes gleaming in the fire's light and his red beard quiver as he spoke with fervor.

"One day we shall plough and plant, harvest and reap in our own land, and we shall live in a house and not in a hut."

The next day, when the wanderers came into an oasis, Deborah's father cut a twig off an acacia tree. Then he took an earthenware vase, filled it with soft earth in which he planted the twig and gave the vase to his daughter. Deborah was overjoyed by this unusual gift. She attended to it with all the love of her young heart, sharing with the plant her meager water rations and protecting the delicate stalk and leaves from the scorching sun in the day and from the sharp cold at night. The sapling, obviously aware of the encompassing attention and love it received, quickly expanded in all directions, shooting forth new twigs and leaves.

"When we arrive in the Promised Land I will transplant my small acacia tree in a grove near our house and it will tell the young and old trees growing there of our wanderings and hardships in the Desert," thought Deborah one night while gazing at the big desert stars with a cheerful look. The higher the acacia plant grew, the more twigs and leaves sprang forth from the young stem, the happier Deborah became. The bleak palor was gone from her cheeks and she now met the hardships of desert life with ease. Even the sandstorms, which disturbed not one hardened wanderer, she took in stride.

One hot day, so hot that the sky and the desert sands seemed to be ablaze, the thirsty and exhausted wanderers came to a wadi, a stream in the desert. The shallow, transparent waters were the very realization of the Hebrews' wishes and dreams. In an instant, multitudes of wanderers lay crouching on the water's edge, sipping thirstily, for they were too impatient to draw the water by pitcher or vase.

Then, like the roaring of a waterfall was heard the noise of angry, disappointed voices as the water was found to be bitter, horribly bitter, and the thirsty men, women and children couldn't quench their thirst. To be so close to the wadi water, to see the sun's rays reflect in it cheerfully, and to feel its damp, pleasant smell and yet not to be able to drink from it! That made the thirst unbearable!

In the cloud of rising dust as other tribes came forward, in the milling around of excited, angry people, many hard and bitter words were heard. The situation almost became mutinous. Suddenly the storm of human protest and anger stopped. A magic whisper went through the unhappy mass of people.

Dry mouths and throats whispered: "Moses!" and "Moses is coming," and all became still, and curious to know what the great liberator and teacher would do.

The human throngs moved aside, a path was opened and Moses appeared on the shore of the wadi. With him was a young, frail brown-haired girl. With one hand Moses caressed the girl's soft hair and in the other he held a heavy earthenware vase with a young acacia tree rising from it.

The girl was Deborah, the daughter of Dan, with her young acacia tree. The tree which had grown tall and sturdy out of the small heap of earth within the earthenware vase thanks to the care and affection of the girl was the one once given to her as a sapling by her father.

"Would you not like the water to turn sweet so that all the people could drink?" asked Moses staring with warm eyes into the girl's lean, windbeaten face.

Deborah looked very small in comparison with the tall, big-faced and long bearded Moses. She stood embarrassed and perplexed and did not know what to say.

Moses continued: "I know what this acacia tree means to you, my child, and how it satisfies your dreams and wishes in the hard desert life. . . . However, I looked in vain for another tree or bush. . . . Alas, nothing grows here, there are only hard rocks and sand. The only tree that can turn the water sweet and still the people's thirst is your small acacia tree. Allow me therefore to throw it into the water. . . ." finished Moses pleadingly.

By now the girl had regained her courage and was able to think. The loss of the beautiful acacia tree was undoubtedly a blow to her. But of what value was this young tree by comparison with the suffering of thousands and thousands of people including the great Moses, her beloved father, and even herself?

"Yes . . . Yes . . ." stuttered Deborah as she looked at the great teacher's kind, wise face, and at the long beard which was as white as light. Followed by thousands of eyes eager to see a wonder, Moses pulled the young tree from its vase and threw it into the water. The wadi answered with a cheerful splash.

"Now go ahead and quench your thirst, but don't hurt one another as there is enough water for everyone!" exclaimed Moses in a loud, solemn voice so that many could hear him. And in no time thousands of parched mouths and throats felt the life-giving goodness of the now tasty water.

Men, women and children drank standing, sitting, or crouching. The hardened Hebrew wanderers of the desert drank abundantly, like camels, for like camels they anticipated waterless days baked by a mercilessly hot sun. When they paused from drinking they spoke with praise of Moses, their liberator, as about a good, protective father, and about the frail, brown-haired girl Deborah, the daughter of Dan, whose love for a plant did so much good for the Children of Israel.

Moses and the Little Sparrow

When food was scarce in the desert and the wandering Hebrews were hungry all the time, manna fell from the sky upon the endless stretches of sand.

Each morning the Israelites came out of their tents and picked up the tasty pieces of manna, which they eagerly ate.

When some of the birds and animals had tasted the manna they developed a liking for it, so that, at times, the Hebrews missed their rations.

When the two mighty kings of the animals and the birds—the lion and the eagle—heard that the manna had been eaten by their kin, they immediately ordered them not to eat it, for the manna was the Hebrews' only food in the desert.

And, to be sure that this order would be obeyed by all creatures, the mighty eagle flew high over the Israelite camp and, with his sharp gaze, followed every move of the birds and animals on the desert sands. The king of the beasts, the lion, watched the animals in the dense thickets or among rocks where the eagle's sharp eye could not reach them.

It is perhaps unnecessary to mention that all the creatures of the desert wished to live in peace with the two mighty rulers, and they dared not break the law.

However, it happened at this time that the only sparrow which lived in the desert, the ever-hungry sparrow, was away drinking in a distant oasis. It knew nothing of the crystal manna which fell each dawn upon the sands and plains of the desert, and of the strict order issued by the eagle and the lion.

Early one morning, when the sparrow winged its way back and saw the glittering crystal pieces of food against the rising sun, it started pecking lustily away at the manna. The eagle spotted this as he was circling high on his patrolling mission. At the sight of a small,weak bird breaking the discipline in the animal world, the eagle became very angry. Full of anger, he swooped down.

In no time the sparrow lay upon the sand helpless and trembling before the mighty eagle. The king of the birds was ready to kill the terror-stricken bird with his sharp, big bill and vicious claws.

At that moment Moses came out of his tent and saw the trembling sparrow at the mercy of the eagle. Moses was filled with compassion and drove off the mighty eagle with his staff. He then took the weak and trembling sparrow into the tent and each day fed it with some of his own manna ration.

When the Children of Israel heard of this they praised the man Moses and loved him more than ever.

The Stony Path

When Moses was ready to climb to the top of Mount Sinai to receive the Ten Commandments engraved on tablets of stone, the paths leading to the mountain top started quarreling with each other. Each path wanted Moses to walk over it.

"I am the shortest way to the mountain top," said one path. "Moses should choose me."

Another path said, "No trail is as smooth and wide as I am. I surely deserve that the great man Moses should walk over me."

"But only I wind beside cool mountain streams," cried still another. "When Moses feels tired he can

drink the refreshing water and then continue on his way to the peak."

"But all along my sides grow rows of tall date trees, their long, leafy branches laden with ripe fruit," rapidly said another path. "The great liberator and teacher will enjoy both the shade and the fruit during his long climb."

There was yet another path which led to the top of the mountain, a narrow trail with many sharp stones. It did not take part in the debate. Silently it yearned to be walked on by Moses, yet it did not dare even to talk about its hopes to the other paths.

"Who am I, that Moses, the Lord's great servant, should walk over me to the mountain top where he will meet God face to face? Why, even the shepherds who come here to graze their sheep avoid me. How could Moses ever, ever choose to walk over my rough stones?" thought the path humbly.

The eyes of Moses filled with a soft thankfulness as he looked at the paths slowly rising through bushes and rocks toward the mysterious heights of the mountain. All had offered themselves to him. But with even more gratitude and warmth did he look at the narrow path which thought so humbly of itself.

Then Moses, silent and motionless, became so lost in thought that he seemed to be part of the mountain and the plain, a rock in this landscape of rocks, stones, and bushes. His mind hovered in the distant, unknown land of the future. A flame of thought sent its light far into the future, which now appeared to him as bright as the desert sands when night has vanished and the dawn is lit by the beams of a new and refreshed sun.

A look of pain appeared on the Liberator's thoughtful face as he saw his people persecuted and oppressed by wicked, Pharaoh-like rulers, driven from one land to another under the whip of hatred and prejudice by merciless tyrants. Moses thought of the difficulties and hardships which his fellow Jews would suffer because of the Laws he was about to receive upon the Tablets of Stone. For he knew that the other tribes and nations would continue to worship their idols and refuse to accept God's laws.

"If my people will one day be oppressed and persecuted because of the Laws which I am about to teach them, how can I take the comfortable path? I must climb the narrow trail which is covered with sharp stones, and thus be united with my brethren who live in distant and difficult times. I want to feel as they will some day feel."

And Moses went up the narrow, stone-covered path. When he reached the top of the mountain he was tired, and the soles of his feet, cut by the sharp stones on the road, were torn and bloody.

But God appeared to him, and he was healed, and his strength returned.

Moses on Mt. Nebo

With a heavy heart Moses climbed to the top of Mt. Nebo. He slowly walked over the narrow path grown with prickly plants and strewn with little stones, pushing away the hard ground with his sturdy staff which had performed so many wonders for the Children of Israel. When he finally reached the top of the mountain he realized how worthwhile the climb was. A beautiful vista, as colorful as a rainbow opened before him. In the clear air of the summer day, Moses saw the blue thread of the Jordan river running through a soft green carpet of valleys and fields, the sun-gilded tips of Judean hills, and white spots of houses peering through some town mosaic. "How beautiful is the Promised Land! What a refreshing view after endless wandering in the wilderness!" Moses exclaimed, feeling the intense beats of his old, tired heart. He sighed as he thought of the long, thorny road leading from Egyptian slavery through fruitless pleading and arguing with the mighty Pharaoh, the punishment in the form of plagues, and finally—the splitting of the waters of the Red Sea, which brought freedom to his people. He thought of days without food and water under a scorching sun, of battles with hostile tribes, of meditation and soul-searching when he had arrived on the top of Mt. Sinai where he met God face to face, and of his return to the Israelite camp after forty days of absence, with the Tablets under his arm.

"A mountain just like this one, and the rocks and stones look almost the same. Yet how elated I felt on Mt. Sinai! I was much younger then, full of vigor and vitality, but above all—the Lord's grace was with me. But now, as I have disobeyed Him, I will never be able to enter Canaan—the Land of our hopes and dreams. And I am now old and tired and my life's task has come to an end. Joshua, whom I brought up and inspired to do great deeds, is young and full of devotion and idealism. The sturdy youths born in the desert in freedom, who never knew the bitter taste of slavery nor the whip of fear, follow the young and brave Joshua. That is the way of life. . . ." A mild breeze caressed his wrinkled face, the long beard as white as light. He looked back at the wilderness surrounding Mt. Nebo, at the familiar view of tents, shacks, and human figures in various forms and shapes, and continued spinning his thoughts: "Forty years of living in the desert are at

an end and a new phase starts for the Children of Israel. Joshua is a brilliant war leader, but will he be equally good in ruling the people in time of peace? And will he be able to fill the gaps between the tribes, erase their superstitious and prejudiced views and fuse them all into a solid oneness? I remember: after we crossed the Red Sea some of us found it difficult to accept the newly gained freedom. . . . Strange as it seems, some Israelites were longing not only for the pots of flesh but even for the clay and bricks, for Pharaoh's guards and whips. . . . However, we are now facing difficulties of another nature. During the long wandering in the wilderness the Hebrews had no reason to love the hot sand and stones over which they walked and lived. Most of the time the desert was hostile to the wanderers. The food came from the sky and rarely from the meager, sandy soil. Now begins a new era. The Land of Canaan is green and good. It will give in abundance of its fruits and water to the Israelites, provided they care for the land, work on it and protect it from enemies. . . . A new love will have to be born in my people's hearts."

Moses rose from the rock on which he sat and again his keen glance hovered past Moabite fields, towards the green carpet of orchards and meadows which were soon to become the possession of the Children of Israel. He sighed as he thought: "I wished I could follow my brethren into Canaan, even for only a short while, and help Joshua in the most difficult task of settling in the Land. Then I would return to the desert to die. . . ."

A small stone rolled down from a nearby rock and stopped at the end of his staff. Moses looked at it curiously and went on: "It was wrong of me to hit the rock. I should have spoken to the rock as God told me to do. One never knows how important a commandment is. I realize I have sinned, and have to be punished. Yet, do I have to be punished so severely, to die in isolation from friends and relations in the land of troubled yesterdays—the wilderness? Is the Lord not capable of forgiving a transgression? Where is His mercy and love? . . ."

But Moses quickly regretted at the thought. "The Lord's ways are hidden from human reason," he went on meditating. "Man's mind is limited and he doesn't understand the meaning of reward and punishment. The thing for me to do is to accept what happens unprotesting, just as in the past I have accepted hunger, thirst, and sandstorms."

He sat down under a small bush. It miraculously rose from under a big rock that seemed to be crushing it with its heavy weight. The short, thin trunk and lean branches told of scanty water and of smiting winds. As the sun shone through it the little leaves looked like tiny flames. Moses thought of the burning bush through which God's voice had spoken to him for the first time.

On Mt. Nebo

When the birds saw Moses standing on the peak of Mt. Nebo gazing towards the Promised Land, they became worried and said to one another: "The great teacher and liberator of the Hebrews is old and tired and if he stands under the hot sun with neither food nor drink, he might become weak. Let us bring him some food and water for, on many days when we had nothing to eat, Moses fed us tasty manna."

The king of the birds—the Eagle—favorably impressed by his subjects' idea, shrieked contentedly: "Splendid! In no time I will pick up a fat mountain sheep and bring it to Moses. He will surely eat it with great relish, and will feel much stronger." "Please don't O king!" For the first time, the doves, swallows, and sparrows dared to contradict the mighty Eagle. "Moses probably will not like the killing of a sheep; he got along for years without eating meat during the wandering in the desert. Surely, he will most appreciate some fruits from trees growing in the Land of Canaan, and water from the beautiful Jordan, because the Holy Land is so dear to him."

The Eagle glanced fiercely at the birds. He realized that they were right, but it was beneath his dignity to admit it. For an instant he thought: they belong to the weakest and most meaningless creatures in his kingdom and their life and death depended on his wish. But he quickly reminded himself of Moses, whom he admired, and he yielded to the birds. He hurried them on with his sharp, domineering voice: "Go on, I have enough of your endless babbling. Do it right away. Hurry!"

"What about us? Can we also do something for Moses?" called several nightingales and canaries who flew in at that very moment. "Of course! You will sing your beautiful songs to make Moses' stay on the Mountain pleasant," replied the doves, sparrows, and swallows and speedily left for the Land of Canaan.

While the singing birds sang their sweet songs to make Moses' stay pleasant, and their feathered brethren were in flight toward Canaan, the mighty Eagle circled in the sky and kept a close watch over the teacher and liberator of the Hebrews who stood alone amidst the huge rocks, and stones, and bushes gazing longingly into the distance, far away. . . . As the flock of birds reached the Holy Land it divided into two groups. One flew towards the hill Moriah upon which, centuries later, Solomon built the Temple, while the other dashed for the waters of the

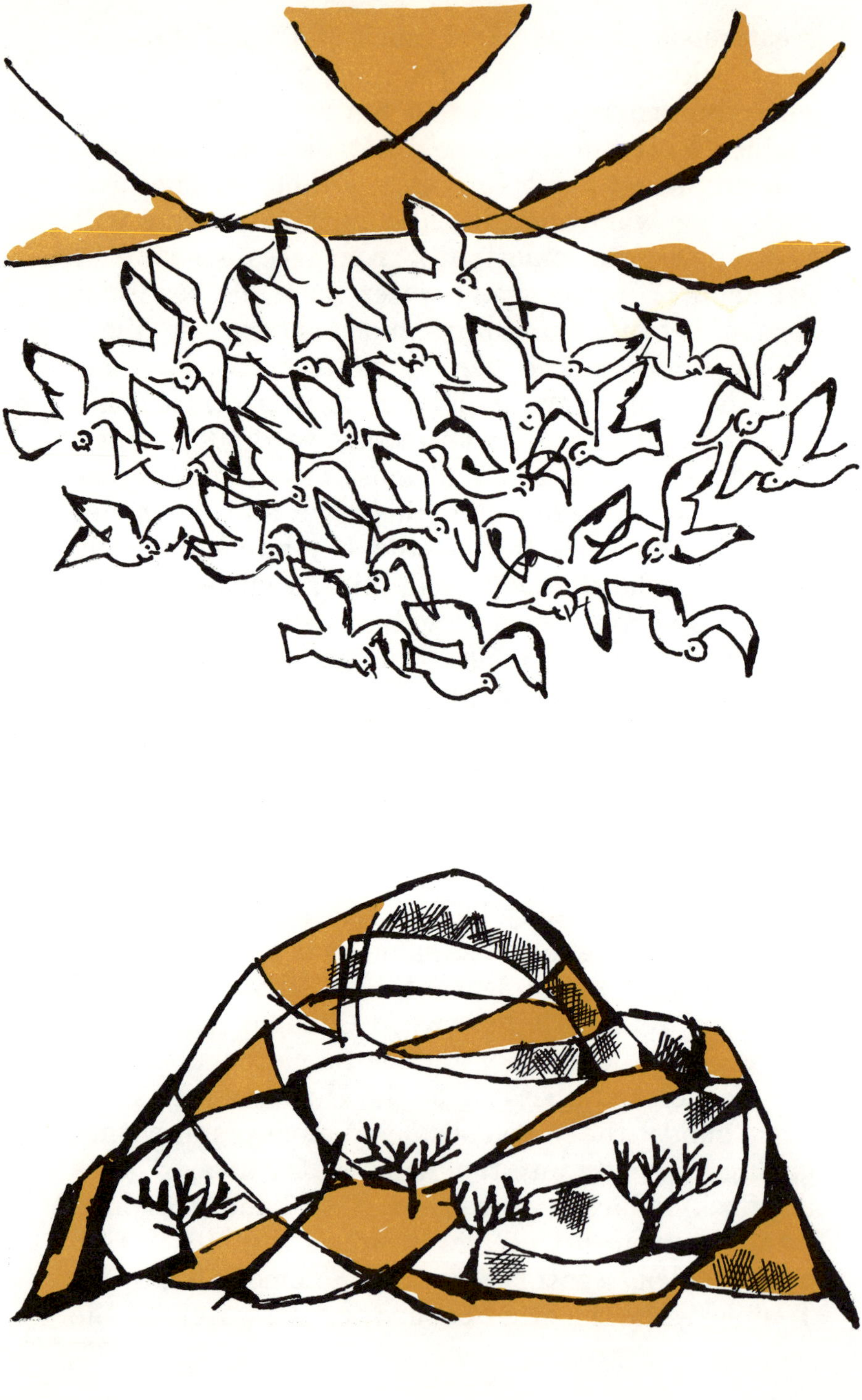

Jordan. On Moriah grew two large fruit trees, on one grew dates and on the other, figs. When the birds descended upon the trees, the branches remained still in the breeze, so that the welcome visitors were able to pluck the fruit quickly. The same thing happened when the birds landed on Jordan's shore. During the day, a strong wind had been blowing and the river was swelling with white-capped waves. As soon as the birds told the Jordan the reason of their coming, the river became calm so that the birds were able swiftly to fill their bills with water. With a cheerful flap of their wings they left the beautiful Jordan and flew back toward Mt. Nebo, just as their fruit-plucking kin did.

Near Moses' feet lay a very old stone, with an almost round depression in its surface, whose hard crust was half washed away by endless rains and scorched by the hot sun until it became dark-brown. The birds landed on the edge of the stone and into the depression dropped the precious gifts they brought. Moses was moved to tears by the goodness of his feathered friends. Eagerly he drank the water from the Jordan river, and gratefully ate the dates and figs that grew on the trees of Moriah. When he blessed the Promised Land he also silently blessed his devoted friends—the birds.

Foolish Balaam and the Wise Donkey

Balaam rode his donkey to the plain on which the Israelites had camped. He intended to curse them, but God gave the animal wisdom and taught it the knowledge of right and wrong.

The donkey thought sadly:

"My master is looked upon as a wise man and a prophet, but he is really weak in character, for he was easily persuaded by Balak, King of Moab, to do a wicked deed. What Balaam wants to do to the Hebrew people, who are proceeding peacefully toward their Promised Land, is a cruel thing.

"I will therefore take him through a lovely part

of the countryside, and when he sees the beauty of the hills and the valleys which God has created, Balaam will also think of God's goodness and will not agree to Balak's wicked plan of cursing the Hebrews."

So the good, sensitive donkey took a road which led through some very graceful countryside.

It was springtime. A light blue sky arched over the valleys and hills, over the fruit-laden almond, fig, and pomegranate trees. When a breeze blew through the air, a rain of petals fell from the blooming trees as if they longed for the earth from which the trees grew and were nourished.

The fragrant scent of spring and earth, mingled with the tender smell of blossoms, filled the air. On a nearby tree, a bird sang with a sweet but sad voice. The bird was happy because spring had arrived, bringing with it much beauty and loveliness. At the same time the songster seemed to be sad, perhaps because the petals were already falling off the trees.

The bird's song was so gentle and delicate that it almost moved the sensitive donkey to tears.

"I am only a donkey and not as wise as man, yet I can feel the glory of the Lord, who in His kindness created all that is beautiful and good to all my senses. I wish that my master felt the same way, so that he could hate no one. Then only friendliness and love would live in his heart," thought the wise and sensitive donkey.

But Balaam was busy thinking of himself, dreaming of the handsome rewards and honors which the warlike Moabite king would give him after he had performed his wicked deed.

It was a warm day, and as the donkey carried Balaam through a village it saw a young man rolling away a huge stone which covered the village well, so that the older men and women standing nearby and waiting eagerly for water might be able to drink.

The donkey, seeing this, thought hopefully:

"I will let my master know that I am thirsty, and when he goes to bring me water he will see how people can be kind to each other. Perhaps that will change him for the better and he will not carry out Balak's plan."

The donkey brayed with a shrill voice, thus announcing its urgent need for water.

But Balaam, instead of bringing water for the donkey, kicked and whipped the well-meaning animal and went on dreaming of wealth and power. With a heavy heart the donkey gave up the idea of improving its master, and regretfully thought about the Israelites who would soon be hurt by Balaam's sharp-tongued curses and thus become an easy prey for Moab's attack.

God pitied the donkey and sent His angel to stand before Balaam with a drawn sword. And, as the Bible tells us, Balaam's plans were changed. The good donkey's hopes came true at last. As Balaam stood on the hill overlooking the orderly Israelite camp, he blessed the Hebrews instead of cursing them.

Moses' Staff

When Moses was about to die he called Joshua into his tent and spoke to him thus: "From now on You will lead the people into the Promised Land as I am soon to die in the wilderness. Now take my staff with which I have performed many miracles and, after you enter Canaan, plant it in its soil as if it were a sapling, for a wondrous date tree will grow out from it."

Joshua was mindful of Moses' wish. He kept the staff with him all the time, in peace and in war, and after the Promised Land was occupied and divided among the Children of Israel, he planted the staff on

Mount Ephraim. And it happened as Moses foretold. As soon as the staff touched the earth it turned into a full-grown, beautiful date tree. The straight trunk rose high above the ground, and the long branches were hung with dark-brown fruit. Tired wanderers who happened to pass by the site, felt refreshed under its shade, and the hungry ate the tasty, juicy dates and blessed the tree.

In the days of the Judges, Deborah the Prophetess, the Judge of the tribe Ephraim, a woman of great valor and ability, sat in the shade of the date tree as it grew near her house, and judged the farmers and shepherds who came flocking to her for advice. And in the cool summer evenings, when the surrounding hills, fields, and orchards were steeped in silence, and the stars were in the heavens, Deborah used to come to the tree alone, to think and meditate, until the soft rustle of the branches and leaves inspired her to create beautiful poems. But one night the tree shook back and forth in the wind as it never had done before, crying with strange voices. Deborah the Prophetess stood at the window in her house and attentively listened. The tree spoke of the brutal, ambitious Canaanite war lord, Sisera, who planned to march against Israel with his vast army of iron chariots, and of the terrible destruction he was able to inflict. Suddenly she saw a bolt of lightning, like a shining knife, cut through the cloudy sky and fall near the house. At the same instant the tree's biggest branch broke off with a great cracking noise, and fell against the door of her house. When she opened the door she found a powerful bow for shooting arrows. . . .

With this very bow the valiant Barak, who led the Israelite army against the Canaanite invaders, killed the horse on which Sisera was riding causing him to

fall into a ravine. Anxious and bewildered Sisera ran from the battlefield and hid in a tent, only to be killed by Deborah's friend. After their commander was gone, the Canaanites became panicky and fled in a disorderly fashion. Deborah expressed Israel's joy and gratitude to the Lord in a famous poem which we know as the Song of Deborah.

Centuries went by. Difficult times came for the Jewish people. Roman soldiers by the thousands roamed through Israel's land. The Holy Temple and Jerusalem lay in ruins. The Roman occupant tried to put out the last lights of religious and national freedom that were left to the Jews. Like one man the people rose to defend the precious remnants of their independence. The heroic Bar Kochba and the scholarly Akiba led the Jewish fighters against the Roman hordes. In a cave that was near the wondrous date tree and through which a tiny spring flowed, a group of Jewish guerrilla fighters had their hiding place. Under cover of night, they made daring forays against the Roman troops which proved costly to the enemy. The Romans cut off all the paths leading to the neighboring villages from which food came to the fighters. Then the juicy fruit of the date tree was the only food that kept the Jewish warriors alive. After each meal they felt strengthened and eager to fight. For months the skirmishes went on and the enemy was unable to make any headway. Finally the Romans sent for reinforcements and the strongly outnumbered Jews were forced to flee into the hills.

When the Romans occupied the site and they saw the tree, heavy with its fruit of ripe dates, they realized how the Jewish fighters had been able to hold out for so long. In a burst of anger they decided to cut down the tree. As it fell the seeds spread with the wind over Israel's whole land. As time passed the seeds sank into the soil, patiently waiting for the return of the rightful owners of this beautiful land. When the modern pioneers returned from the Diaspora and tilled the Israeli earth with devotion and love, the seeds burst forth into saplings, and these grew into graceful date trees.

Joshua and the Sun

After the death of Moses, Joshua became the leader of the Children of Israel. He led our people into the Promised Land. But there were enemies who resisted the march of the Israelites. Joshua waged many battles against the foe, and little by little, the land of Canaan became the land of Israel. One town after another fell to the victorious Joshua and his brave men.

One day, the sun, beaming down on the plains of Jordan, beheld the tribe known as the Amorites fleeing before the Israelites in great confusion. The sun grew fearful of Joshua and said to itself:

"Those Amorites are my faithful followers. They worship me! I am their god. They sing my praises morning and night. Now they are being wiped out by the Israelites. Soon the Children of Israel will occupy the whole land and there will be no one left to bow down and pray to me!"

A cloud darkened the face of the sun. "These Hebrews!" it mused. "They have wandered for many years in the wilderness. They're nomads, that's all. They don't know how to appreciate my beauty, nor are they thankful for the great good I do in the world. Instead of revering me, they bow and pray to a God of Justice and Righteousness who can't even be seen or heard.

"I shall take away my light from Joshua and the Children of Israel so that they will not see how to conquer my devoted worshippers. Though it is the middle of the day, I will set! The Israelites will have to fight in the darkness. Ha! Joshua and his warriors fight well enough when I generously give my light, but they will not do half as well in the darkness. Let them lose the battle!"

And the sun suddenly began to slip into the west. As it set, a pale moon appeared over the plains of Jordan.

Now a fear overwhelmed the Israelites. Never had they seen such a strange sight. The advance guard broke ranks and retreated in haste.

The Amorites, on the other hand, greeted the sun's setting with shouts of gratitude and joy. They thought that the sun-god was coming to their aid. This would turn the tide of battle against the Israelites, they thought. So they rushed courageously into the attack.

But Joshua refused to yield so easily. "There is something odd about the sun today," he said. "It goes

down too soon and too speedily. I sense danger. I'd better stop the sun right now!"

Then, standing on top of a hill and watching the sun's westward progress with worried eyes, Joshua remembered the promise which God had given. The Children of Israel **would inherit Canaan,** He had said. Whereupon Joshua took fresh courage, and in a clear, steady voice filled with confidence and faith, he exclaimed: "Sun, stand still upon Gibeon; and you, Moon, in the valley of Aijalon!"

No sooner had the words come out of Joshua's mouth than the sun trembled and stood still in its place.

Ashamed and helpless, the sun thought: "I am not as powerful as I thought I was. The God of the Children of Israel and of all human beings is also the master over light and darkness. The truth is that He is also **my** God and I am only a small part of His creation. It must be the will of God that the Israelites win the war and inherit the Promised Land."

So the sun chased away all the clouds and shone on the plains of Jordan until Joshua and his people had conquered the Amorites. When the battle was over and the Israelites were weary but victorious, the sun went down.

Samson's Advice

One day Samson happened to come into a village. As soon as the villagers found out who the important visitor was, they rejoiced and prepared a lavish feast for him. When he had finished eating and drinking, the villagers crowded around to beseech him for advice. The village Elder, a white-bearded, distinguished-looking man, stepped forward and said: "Samson, we have heard that God has bestowed upon you immense strength with which you harass our deadly enemy, the Philistines. Just yesterday, the Philistine oppressors, after terrorizing our community for a long time, fled from here in fear when

they found out you were coming. But before leaving they dug a deep pit in which they buried all the gold, silver, and other valuables. Then they covered the treasures with a large rock, intending some day to come back for them. This morning we all assembled and tried to roll the rock away from the pit, but we couldn't budge it by even one inch. The rock is as heavy as a small mountain. We therefore beg of you, Samson, to use your tremendous strength and roll that rock away."

Samson stared for a moment at the Elder's milk-white beard, at the deep wrinkles on his sun-browned face which told of hard toil and suffering under the Philistine yoke. Then the powerful giant looked at the silent crowd of men, women and children who waited to hear what he would say. "Why do you need the Philistine's gold and silver? Is it that important to you?" asked Samson. "Your honor, the gold and silver are ours. The enemy burst into our homes and seized it," quickly replied the Elder. Samson smiled gently at the beseeching Elder who clasped his hands as if in prayer and at the circle of people around him and finally said: "Well, let us go. Lead me to that rock."

They all went to the foot of the mountain where a great boulder seemed cemented to the earth itself. Samson approachd and said: "This is it?" The villagers answered in one voice: "Yes, yes, this is the rock rolled over our treasures by the Philistines." Samson spread his arms against the face of the boulder and with a mighty push of his arms and shoulder muscles he shoved it away from the pit. With a joyous cry the villagers rushed up to retrieve their buried treasure. Their hands flew to get at the gold and silver, and in a few moments there were cries of anguish and disappointment. Their treasures were no longer in the pit. "A Philistine trick!" they moaned. "Our gold and silver have been carried off by our enemies!" Then Samson began digging with his hands and brought up some Philistine swords and spears. He raised the weapons high against the sun and told them: "This my brethren, is your treasure, and not gold and silver. Gold and silver can do nothing for you, but with swords and spears you will be able to defend your lives and your homes, your fields and your dignity."

The villagers glanced at one another and their eyes shone with a new understanding. Their faces hardened with a look of firmness and pride as Samson was saying to them: "And now, take these war tools and learn how to use them. Some day, when the enemy will try to force his yoke upon you again, you will know how to fight for your freedom and your lives." Then the great Hebrew thanked the villagers for their hospitality. He raised both arms in a gesture of love and encouragement. He was still smiling when he turned away and, with a final wave of farewell, strode from their midst.

Samson's Friends

The judge Samson, famous for his unusual strength and heroic fighting against the Philistines, loved the fields and woods, the valleys and mountains of his homeland. But above all Samson loved birds. He fed them and protected their nests from beasts of prey. The birds loved Samson too, and rejoiced in his courageous deeds. They said:

"The Philistines will not dare to plunder Israel's fields and vineyards any longer. Our nests are now safe, and we can fly freely and sing about our beautiful land."

And of all the birds, it was the mountain eagle who

loved Samson most.

"I am the strongest and the most daring among the birds, as Samson is the strongest and bravest of men!" the eagle proudly exclaimed from his mountain-top nest.

One day sad news reached the birds. Samson's wife, Delilah, was cutting off her husband's hair, the source of his miraculous strength, so that he would no longer be able to fight the Philistines.

The birds instantly flew towards Delilah's house, and looking through the small window in the wall, saw Samson's long hair falling under Delilah's quick, sharp scissors while he lay asleep. Seeing this, the birds began to twitter and shriek with all their might, trying to wake their beloved friend and hero. But Samson was deep in sleep and could not hear the voices of the birds.

"Samson is in danger. Who will fly in to wake him up?" screeched the bluejay.

"I! I!" angrily screamed the eagle.

But the huge mountain eagle could not get through the small window, and he fell to the ground, hurting his wings.

"Who, then, can wake Samson up? Hurry!" again exclaimed the bluejay.

The big, gleaming scissors in the hand of Delilah frightened the birds and for a short while they sat on the rooftop of the house thinking of what to do.

"I will wake him up!" said the swallow, and darted into the house, swift as an arrow.

Thrice did the bird touch Samson's face with its soft blue wings.... Finally he woke up from his deep sleep. Tired and weakened he tried to rise from the bed. But at this very moment the last lock of his long, glorious hair fell to the floor . . . and the startled, unhappy swallow beheld several armed Philis-

tines pounce upon Samson and bind him with heavy brass chains.

Blinded and chained, Samson stood between the two pillars of the Philistine temple of Dagon. In despair he thought of the Hebrew shepherds and farmers who would have no defender. Then he heard a soft flutter of bird's wings. His friends the birds had come to free him! One after another they swooped down and pecked at the ugly chains with their bills. . . . **"Clink-clong!"** the links angrily clanked each time the birds hit them with their bills. Alas! The birds' bills were too weak to break the heavy brass chains. But Samson felt better and a trace of a smile appeared on his troubled face.

"I am not alone. My friends, the birds, have not forsaken me even now, while my enemies are getting ready to put me to death!" Samson whispered to himself. And he bent his head in prayer to God. "Let me revenge myself on these Philistines!" he prayed.

Suddenly, new courage filled his body, and he pushed at the pillars of the temple of Dagon, the god of the Philistines, with all his strength. When the temple fell by the power of Samson's mighty arms, killing him along with hundreds of his enemies, the birds circled for a long time over his body in a mood of mourning and solemn silence. In this way they paid last honors to their beloved friend.

The Broken Tablets

After Moses had broken the Tablets bearing the Ten Commandments, the shattered pieces of stone complained bitterly to God.

"Lord of the Universe!" they said. "For long centuries did we await the coming of Moses. We did not mind the howling winds, nor the stabbing lightning, nor the scorching sun, for we cherished a great dream. Do we now deserve this harsh punishment? Is it our fault that during the time that Moses was on Mt. Sinai some of the Israelites made a golden calf and worshipped it?"

Silence swept the sandy plain, the long rows of Israelite tents, and towering Mount Sinai. Then the voice of God was heard:

"O fragments of stone, you are dearer to me than ever before, for it was not your sin that caused you to be broken. And because you were faithful, I promise that one day you will have an important task to fulfill."

A strong wind began to blow. It picked up the stone fragments and carried them towards Jerusalem, which was then a Jebusite town in Canaan. And all the pieces of stone, except one with very sharp edges, dropped on a mountain named Moriah, in the heart of Jerusalem.

The sharp-edged fragment was borne westward by the wind to,the valley of Elah.

Years and generations and centuries passed. Then. one day, a brave shepherd boy named David picked up a sharp piece of stone, put it in his sling, and with all his strength aimed it at the Philistine giant Goliath, who had mockingly challenged the Israelites.

"I must hit Goliath and save the Hebrews!" whispered the fragment, for it was indeed the keen-edged piece of the broken Tablets. And it sped through the air and sank into the giant's forehead.

That day our people won a great victory and a stalwart shepherd began his rise to greatness and fame.

Quite a different fate awaited the fragments on Mount Moriah. For a long time they unhappily watched the pagan idol worship of the Jebusites. When David occupied the city and turned it into the capital of Israel, they were happy.

One day, at King Solomon's command, workmen climbed Moriah to build the Holy Temple. By then the splinters and chips of the Tablets had become part of a single rock, fused together by time, rain, and sun. This rock was used as one of the cornerstones of God's House. Thus, finally, did all the pieces of the broken Tablets fulfill their task as the Lord had foretold.

The Lebanese Hawk

Hiram, the King of Phoenicia, a land famous for its able builders and daring seafarers, was on very friendly terms with King Solomon.

When Solomon was ready to build the Holy Temple in Jerusalem, Hiram sent him architects and engineers. He also brought into Jerusalem tall, stately cedar trees from the forests of Lebanon to be used as building material. As a sign of gratitude, the Jewish farmers and shepherds sent flocks of sheep and cattle, and agricultural products to the friendly Phoenicians.

One day the Phoenician king honored Solomon's

lieutenant with a rare gift—a wild Lebanese hawk. The bird was highly valued by its owner, not only because of the importance of its sender but also for its great speed in flying and the unusual multicolored beauty of its feathers. Even King Solomon, whose taste was very fine in matters of beauty and art, admired the hawk.

However, no sooner had the bird arrived in Jerusalem than many pigeons in the neighboring villages began to disappear as if by magic, and the villagers, at first in secret and then in public, complained that their pigeons were being killed by the rare Lebanese hawk.

The farmers went to see the king's lieutenant and politely pointed out their losses to him and asked him to keep the hawk caged.

But the lieutenant refused to listen and grew very angry. He met the complaints of the villagers with an angry outburst:

"How dare you blame this hawk of mine? It is absolutely innocent! Besides, do you know that it is a gift from Hiram, Phoenicia's great king! It comes from a royal home. Do you think that I feed it so little that it is driven to live on peasants' pigeons? Out, out, out!"

And the king's lieutenant dismissed the group of villagers from his house.

Having received no satisfaction, and believing their complaint to be justified, the humble farmers decided to take the problem to King Solomon himself, for he was known as a just and wise ruler.

The king listened carefully to both sides and after a while he turned to his lieutenant and asked:

"Can the graceful mountain hawk be brought into the palace?"

"Certainly, O King!" replied the lieutenant with a

triumphant smile. He felt certain that because of his high rank, the king would side with him.

The king's keen eyes looked at the bird's beautiful feathers but they also noted the hawk's sharp talons and beak. Then Solomon whispered to his nearest servant. The servant disappeared for a short time. When he returned, he carried a white dove which he released in the center of the throne room. It soared high above the heads of the people gathered in the immense hall.

At this instant the Hawk which perched on the table near the lieutenant, flew like an arrow from a bow toward the defenseless dove. With savage strength it pounced upon the poor bird, ready to sink its sharp beak and talons into it.

In a twinkling, the palace was filled with shrieks and noise and flying feathers.

Then, at the order of the king, servants dashed forward. They saved the dove from death, and put the lieutenant's hawk into a cage.

When silence had fallen on the gathering, the king spoke in a calm, clear voice.

"It is easy to see who is right and who is wrong. My own lieutenant will therefore pay the villagers for the losses they have suffered, and from now on this beautiful Lebanese hawk will have to stay in its cage."

The villagers left the palace with a great feeling of satisfaction, and they praised the name of their wise and just king.

King Solomon and the Dove

King Solomon was known for his great wisdom and knowledge. He not only knew the languages of most nations and tribes, but he also understood the languages of the birds and the animals.

When he was free from his royal duties, the king walked or rode through the fields and forests close to Jerusalem and listened eagerly to the chatter of the animals and the birds.

King Solomon admired most of the creatures, some for their beauty and others for their cleverness. But, above all, he loved the mild and beautiful doves.

One day, as he walked through a field, he heard

one dove telling another in a distressed coo how it had just flown over a valley and had seen a battle raging between the inhabitants of two villages. The wounded and killed were strewn over the battlefield.

The king, who hated war and bloodshed, listened carefully and at once decided to stop this senseless slaughter. He quickly returned to the palace and ordered his servants to harness his chariot with his fastest horses, and he dashed off to the valley where the fighting was taking place.

When the combatants saw that the king had come, they stopped fighting, threw away their weapons and bowed in reverence to the unexpected royal visitor.

King Solomon came down from his chariot and spoke to the people. He pointed out to them how painful and destructive war was and on the other hand, how pleasant and constructive it was to work and live in peace with one's neighbors.

He then made peace between the villagers and ordered them to bury the dead, attend the wounded, and help the widowed and orphaned. On the way home the king thought hard about how important it was to educate people to love peace and to hate war, so he decided to build a House of God, where men and women from near and far, rich and poor, countrymen and city dwellers, could come to pray and, through their prayers, learn to love peace.

In time, the king realized his dream and built the Holy Temple on Mount Moriah, known under the Hebrew name of Bet Hamikdash.

The Prophet Elijah and the Deer

Elijah once walked near the Jordan River and saw a young deer being attacked by a wolf. The deer bravely tried to fight off the wolf with its sharp antlers and by quick kicks of its legs. But it was obvious that the tender creature, already hurt by the wolf's fangs, was quickly tiring and that it would soon lose its battle for its life.

Elijah felt sorry for the poor deer.

"One of the most tender animals created by the Lord is in danger of being destroyed by brute force," thought the Prophet. He immediately ran toward the wolf and chased it off with his heavy oaken staff.

Then he led the bleeding, trembling deer into one of the caves which often served him as a home. He treated its wounds with herbs and water from the Jordan and then brought some food for it from the nearby valley.

Elijah nursed the deer until the wounds healed, and led it into a dense part of the woods where it felt safe. Then he left on his way to Samaria, to spread the word of the eternal God.

On the edge of the city a poor sick widow lived in a small shabby house. Her husband had been killed defending the country against its neighbor, Aram. Her two daughters worked as servants in the palace of the royal couple Ahab and Jezebel.

Whenever Elijah came to Samaria he used to visit the poor sick woman, bringing food and healing herbs from the Jordan valley, and a tender, comforting word. In this house Elijah was informed of the doings in the royal palace, and whether the priests of the idol Baal had become more powerful among the people or not. Under the low but hospitable roof of the widow's house, Elijah planned his battles for the One God, for righteousness and for justice.

One day the wicked rulers of Samaria found out that the Prophet Elijah was staying in the widow's house. They promptly sent their guards to encircle the house and capture Elijah, for as long as he moved freely among the people, the royal couple felt insecure.

However, because of his alertness, he escaped before the brutal guards closed in on him.

Elijah fled from the heavily guarded capital of the Kingdom of Israel, which had lately fallen under a new spell of injustice, misery and idol-worshipping. He walked through the surrounding fields towards the villages on the shore of the Jordan River, where

the kind and faithful fishermen and farmers were always ready to welcome him with love, bread, and shelter.

Suddenly he heard the even, rapid sounds of horses' hoofs. Elijah turned. A band of horsemen loomed darkly against the bright blue sky. There was no doubt in the Prophet's mind that these were the mounted guards of Ahab and Jezebel who were pursuing him. Their long spears looked like stalks of wheat against the sky.

"In no time they will be here; where shall I hide?" thought Elijah as he looked in vain for some cave or thicket on the open plain which stretched evenly on all sides as far as the eye could see.

Then something happened which amazed even Elijah, although his life was full of miraculous escapes from the tyrant's powerful hand. Near him there suddenly appeared a tall, beautifully developed deer, and as it knelt down, it looked pleadingly with its soft eyes at Elijah. The prophet quickly mounted upon the deer's back and as it dashed like lightning over plains, hills and valleys, Elijah thought about the brave young deer which he had once saved from the wolf's fangs.

In Naboth's Vineyard

King Ahab and Queen Jezebel of Sidonia were wicked rulers, as the Bible tells us. One day the country was stirred by the cruel death of a farmer, named Naboth, whose vineyard had been seized by the King and Queen.

When the sad news reached the vineyard, the trees felt sorrow and anger. In the strong wind, many voices of protest were heard.

"Naboth was murdered! our rightful and devoted owner!" exclaimed a blooming grapevine as in grief it dropped its clusters of grapes.

A vine near the outer fence moaned: "In the heat of the day he watered us and in the cool nights he protected our grapes from foxes and thieves."

In another part of the vineyard a vine shook its branches angrily and said:

"Honest Naboth was stoned by order of the King and Queen."

Then all the vines grew quiet as the eldest among them spoke:

"King Ahab and Queen Jezebel now own the vineyard. Soon the King's servants will come to pick our grapes. Over the wine made from our fruit, blessings will be chanted to idols instead of to the God of Israel and of the whole world. Brothers and sisters! Let us all shed our fruit so that it may not fall into the royal pickers' hands!"

"You are right!" replied the vines. And they rustled restlessly in the growing wind until their grapes had fallen to the ground.

One exception was a young vine which grew in a sheltered corner of the arbor. Gaily, he said:

"All my life I dreamed of the day when from my grapes wine would be pressed to be served in the royal palace. Now my dream will come true."

How disappointed were Ahab's servants when they came to pick the grapes, for all they saw were empty vines. Then they beheld the young vine which still bore fruit. Eagerly they started to pick the grapes. Suddenly, from the valley of the Jordan a flock of ravens appeared. These were no ordinary black birds. They were the very ravens which, at God's command, had fed the Prophet Elijah with flesh and bread when he was a fugitive.

To the amazement of the royal servants, they swooped down upon the solitary vine, covering it with their flapping black wings. In a moment they had eaten all the grapes. Then they flew away, leaving a mourning vineyard and a royal couple whose punishment for evil deeds had now only begun.

The Persian Wind

When, on the order of King Nebuchadnezzar, the Babylonian hordes invaded Judah and Jerusalem and put the Temple on fire, a wind—the same light wind that used to wake up King David in the dawn by stirring the strings of his harp making it play beautiful, moving melodies—fought the flames with all its might. It dashed from one part of the burning structure to another trying to put out the raging fires that were devouring the House of God. However with each minute the flames, fed by oil which the pagan enemy had poured on the walls of the Temple, became bigger and bolder and, as if realizing their

strength, they quickly spread. From the lower parts of the walls they crawled higher and higher until their red and brilliant fingers took hold of the roof. "How do you dare to destroy God's House?" cried the wind in despair, but the flames laughed with a cynical laughter and went on with their destructive work. The wind then rushed away to find its brethren, the powerful winds that had once brought hailstorms over Egypt and helped split the waters of the Red Sea. But when they came, it was too late, and the Bet Hamikdash was one huge pile of fire and smoke.

Soaring through columns of smoke against a red-lit sky, the wind protested to God: "What now, O Lord?" "You shall follow the exiles into Babylon," said the Lord. And the wind went with the long lines of Judea's brave captives, men and women who had unsuccessfully resisted Nebuchadnezzar's attack. The wind kept the clouds of dust away from them and cooled them from the scorching sun.

Many years went by. The Babylonians, who at one time were the most powerful nation in the Middle East, became corrupt and weak. Their vast Empire fell under the rule of the fresh and vigorous Persians led by the great and wise king, Cyrus. After his death a line of kings and emperors of smaller stature followed. One of them was Ahasureus.

One night the Emperor Ahasuerus was restless and could not fall asleep. "Lavish feasts occupy most of my time. The rule of my vast kingdom is actually in the hands of my chief adviser Haman, and I am not even aware of the most important events which have taken place since I became king," Ahasuerus reproached himself. This thought made the Emperor even more restless and he tried anew, but in vain, to fall asleep. Then he ordered the Book of the Chronicles to be brought to his bedside.

The servant who fulfilled the king's wish was a man of low morals and an admirer of the wicked and powerful Haman to whom he gave full support in his base plans against the Jewish-Persian community. When the King Ahasuerus commanded him to read from the Book, the servant turned to a page depicting Haman's wisdom and valor. Hardly had the servant opened his mouth when the same wondrous wind entered the palace and with all its might blew at the book. The stirred pages turned back and forth as if they wished to fly away. Then the wind was gone.

Silence fell over the palace and the servant now noticed regretfully that the page about Haman had disappeared and in its place lay a page telling of a Jew's devotion to the king and country.

"How long do I have to wait for your reading? Are you not familiar with the alphabet?" asked the king in an angry, sneering tone.

"Your Majesty the King, forgive my transgression, . . ." humbly muttered the servant and bent low. And with a voice not his own he read the story of Mordecai who had saved the king's life when plotters conspired to kill him. Ahasuerus listened attentively and obviously was impressed by the story.

As we all know, since that memorable night events took a turn in favor of the community of Jews in Persia whom the wicked Haman and his followers wanted to destroy.